MY FIRST BOOK OF
Korean Words

an ABC Rhyming Book

Henry J. Amen IV and Kyubyong Park
illustrated by Aya Padrón

TUTTLE Publishing

Tokyo │ Rutland, Vermont │ Singapore

Preface

The words profiled in this book are all commonly used in the Korean language and—we hope you'll agree—are both informative and fun for English-speaking children to learn.

The goals of *My First Book of Korean Words* are multiple: to familiarize children with the sounds and structure of Korean speech; to introduce core elements of Korean culture; to illustrate the ways in which languages differ in their treatment of everyday sounds; and to show how, through cultural importation, a single word can be shared between languages.

That's why, in these pages, you'll encounter words like *dal* (moon) and *nolda* (to play), which signify objects and actions children are familiar with regardless of their mother tongue. We've included terms specific to Korea that carry with them a deeper cultural meaning, like *hanbok* (traditional Korean clothing) and *ondol* (Korean heating system). Words such as *echwi* ("achoo!") and *yaong* (meow) teach that foreign ears often interpret sounds in different ways, while *roket* (rocket) and *sillopon* (xylophone) illuminate how English has influenced languages the world over.

You'll notice that the English letters F, L*, Q, V, X, and Z are not used in the standard Romanization of the Korean alphabet (Hangeul). For these, we've chosen to introduce the Korean equivalents of English words that begin with these letters.

And finally, a few notes on pronunciation for the readers of *My First Book of Korean Words*:

Basic Vowels
A – pronounced "ah"
E – pronounced "eh"
I – pronounced "ee"
O – pronounced "oh"
U – pronounced "oo"
AE – pronounced "eh"

Consonants
G – pronounced hard, as in "girl"
KK – pronounced more sharply than a single "K"
SI – pronounced "shee"

Korean is spoken by 78 million people all over the world. We hope that, with the help of this book, that figure will soon be 78 million +1!

* In actuality, the letter "L" is used in Romanized Hangeul, but it never appears at the beginning of a word.

아침

A is for *achim*.
My **breakfast** is nice—
a cool glass of water
and a big bowl of rice.

In Korea, people like all kinds of food
for breakfast—even veggies! Would you
eat rice and veggies for breakfast?

1

바다 **B** is for *bada*, a **sea** deep and wide.
Korea sticks out and has one on each side.

축구 **C** is for *chukgu*. I play **soccer** with friends.
We watch the World Cup and cheer for Korea to win.

D is for *dal*,
the **moon** shining bright.
I think it's a rabbit
who visits each night.

In Korea and other East Asian countries,
people say there's a rabbit in the moon in the
same way that we say there's a man in the moon.

에 취

E is for *echwi*!
(Excuse me, please.)
This is the sound that
we make when we sneeze.

**Different languages have different
words for sounds. You say "achoo!"
but Koreans say "echwi!"**

날다 **F** is for **flying**—*nalda*, we say.
I fly in my dreams–whoosh!
Up, up, and away!

The English language has some letter sounds that the Korean language doesn't have. The F sound is one of those.

6

김치

G is for the *gimchi*
we eat with each meal—
made from cabbage or radish,
it's so spicy you'll squeal!

Gimchi (also called Kimchi) is the most
famous dish in Korea. It's served with
every meal—even breakfast!

한복

H is for *hanbok*,
our colorful finery.
I wear it on New Year's
and to weddings with family.

Hanbok is the name given to traditional Korean clothing. Long ago, it was worn every day, but now it's worn mainly on special occasions.

이야기   **I** is for *iyagi*, what Grandpa will tell
when I ask for a **story**. He tells them so well!

자장가

J is for *jajangga*, a **lullaby** for me.
Mom sings one each night so I sleep peacefully.

까치

K is for *kkachi*,
the lovely **magpie**.
I put out some birdseed
and hope he'll stop by.

The magpie is a special bird in Korea.
People think it brings good luck when it sings.

L is for **lamb**,
a young little sheep.
In Korean it's *yang*—
isn't she sweet?

There is an L sound in the
Korean language, but it's never
used at the beginning of words.

M is for *mogyok.*
A **bath** makes me calm.
I go to the bathhouse
with Sister and Mom.

목욕

In many Asian countries, like Korea and Japan, people take relaxing baths in public bathhouses.

놀다 **N** is for *nolda*, what I do every day.
Won't you come join me? It means "**to play**"!

온돌

O is for *ondol*.
When it's cold outdoors,
our house is kept warm
by the heat in our floors.

**Ondol is a heater under the floor that
uses hot water or air to warm the home.
It's been used in Korea for 3,000 years!**

팽이

P is for *paengi*,
a toy **top** that spins.
Round, round they all go.
The last one up wins!

Paengi are small tops with a sharp point to spin on. Kids keep them spinning by striking them with long strings.

16

왕비

Q is for **queen**.
We call her *wangbi*.
Look closely, now—
do you recognize me?

**Did you guess that the Korean
language doesn't have a Q sound?**

로 켓

R is for *roket*.
I fly to the moon,
but please don't worry—
I'll fly back again soon.

**Many languages share and
borrow words. Korean
borrows "roket" from the
English word "rocket."**

세 다

S is for *seda*. **Counting** is fun,
forwards or backwards—three, two, one, none!

태권도

T is for **Taekwondo**.
It helps me stay strong
in body and mind.
Can you follow along?

Koreans created Taekwondo
for fighting, but it's also
great exercise!

우산   **U** is for *usan*. Rain falls from the sky,
but my trusty **umbrella** keeps me comfy and dry.

야채

V is for **vegetables**,
the *yachae* on my plate.
Cabbage, carrot, zucchini—
dessert has to wait.

**Korean doesn't have a V sound,
but Korea has plenty of vegetables.**

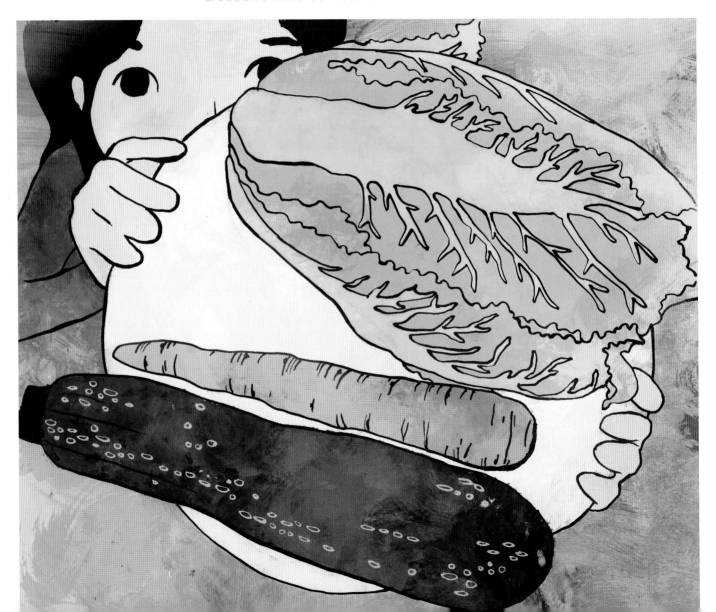

W is for *won*.
That's the money we use.
I saved up my won
to buy fancy new shoes.

원

**Different countries use
different kinds of money.
What money does your
country use?**

실 로 폰

X is for **xylophone**.
It sounds really cool!
We call it a *sillopon*.
I play one at school.

The X sound doesn't exist in Korean, but "xylophone" and "sillopon" sound a lot alike, don't they?

24

야옹

Y is for *yaong*,
what Korean cats say.
My cat Nabi cries "Yaong!"
when she wants me to play.

We hear cats say "meow,"
but Koreans hear "yaong."
What do you think they say?

붕

Z is for **zoom**—
bung! goes the airplane.
I have to go now,
but I'll see you again!

"Zoom" is fun to say, but Korean doesn't
have a Z sound. Kids in Korea say
"bung!" instead. That's fun, too!